Cartoons by Roland Fiddy

The Fanatic's Guide to

COMPUTERS

EXLEY

In the same series:
The Fanatic's Guide to Cats
The Fanatic's Guide to Diets
The Fanatic's Guide to Dogs
The Fanatic's Guide to Golf
The Fanatic's Guide to Men
The Fanatic's Guide to Money
The Fanatic's Guide to Sex

First published in Great Britain in 1991 by
**Exley Publications Ltd, 16 Chalk Hill,
Watford, Herts WD1 4BN, United Kingdom.**

Copyright © Roland Fiddy, 1991

ISBN 1-85015-271-3

Typeset by Brush Off Studios, St Albans, Herts AL3 4PH.
Printed and bound in Hungary.

The computer fanatic knows that computers are INFALLIBLE ...

... it is the Human Factor that messes things up.

The computer fanatic is a serious person – some might say obsessional.

The computer fanatic knows that one can only get __OUT__ of a computer what has been put __IN__ ...

... what has been put IN ...

... what has been put IN ...

... *what has been put __IN__* ...

*... what has been put **IN** ...*

The computer fanatic must be familiar with the language –
e.g. BINARY NUMBERS ...

... BOOLEAN ALGEBRA, BUFFERS, BUGS, BYTES, NIBBLES, PIXELS, PEAKS, POKES, SPRITES, STRINGS ... The rest of us sometimes feel that we are being left behind ...

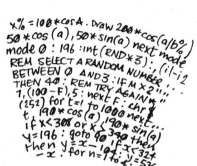

The computer fanatic knows that computers are a
BASIC NECESSITY in business ...

GET RID OF IT!
THERE IS NO ROOM
FOR PESSIMISTS
IN THIS COMPANY!

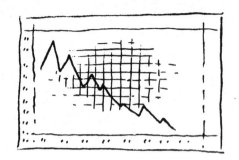

i. NOAH AND THE ARK

IMAGINARY COMPUTER ERRORS IN HISTORY.

2. THE TEN COMMANDMENTS

3. THE BUILDING OF THE PYRAMIDS

4. EINSTEIN PERFECTING HIS THEORY
OF RELATIVITY.

6. TUTANKHAMEN

IMAGINARY COMPUTER ERRORS IN HISTORY.

7. COLUMBUS DISCOVERS AMERICA.

Computer fanatics do not believe that selecting a partner should be left to blind chance or romantic whim.

Our leisure will never be the same again!

Time itself has been computerized!

Roland Fiddy

Roland Fiddy, Cartoonist.

Born in Plymouth, Devon. Studied art at Plymouth and Bristol Colleges of Art. Works as a freelance cartoonist and illustrator. His cartoons have been published in Britain, the United States, and many other countries. Has taken part in International Cartoon Festivals since 1984, and has won the following awards.

1984 Special Prize, Yomiuri Shimbun, Tokyo.

1984 First Prize, Beringen International Cartoon Exhibition, Belgium

1984 Prize of the Public, Netherlands Cartoon Festival.

1985 First Prize, Netherlands Cartoon Festival

1985 "Silver Hat" (Second Prize) Knokke-Heist International Cartoon Festival, Belgium.

1986 First Prize, Beringen International Cartoon Exhibition, Belgium

1986 First Prize, Netherlands Cartoon Festival

1986 First Prize, Sofia Cartoon Exhibition, Bulgaria.

1987 Second Prize, World Cartoon Gallery, Skopje, Yugoslavia.

1987 "Casino Prize" Knokke-Heist International Cartoon Festival, Belgium

1987 UNESCO Prize, Gabrovo International Cartoon Biennial, Bulgaria.

1987 First Prize, Piracicaba International Humour Exhibition, Brazil.

1988 "Golden Date" award, International Salon of Humour, Bordighera, Italy.

1988 Second Prize, Berol Cartoon Awards, London, England.

1989 E.E.C. Prize, European Cartoon Exhibition, Kruishoutem, Belgium.

1989 Press Prize, Gabrovo International Cartoon Biennial, Bulgaria.

1990 First Prize, Knokke-Heist International Cartoon Festival, Belgium.

1991 Prize for Excellence, Yomiuri Shimbun, Tokyo.

The 'Fanatics' series £2.99 (paperback)
The **Fanatic's Guides** are perfect presents for everyone with a hobby that has got out of hand.... Cartoons by Roland Fiddy.

The Fanatic's Guide to Cats
A must for cat lovers everywhere who cannot fail to find fun and laughter in the frolics of our feline friends.

The Fanatic's Guide to Dads
A loving gift for a funny Dad – and fun for all the family. "Dad, I'll be good for the next twenty years if I can have an ice-cream!"

The Fanatic's Guide to Diets
Sixty percent of women are either on a diet – or breaking a diet. Men are surprisingly fanatical too. This is Roland Fiddy's sympathetic laugh at life for the majority of us who keep popping out at the waist.

The Fanatic's Guide to Dogs
Remember that magical word "W-A-L-K-I-E-S"!! This fanatic's guide will lead all dog lovers to stitches and have them collared before they can say "stay".

The Fanatic's Guide to Golf
This is the one gift that the golfer will love.

The Fanatic's Guide to Money
Money makes the world go around – this hilarious book will appeal to the haves and have-nots alike.

The Fanatic's Guide to Sex
Now this is one that you won't give to Aunt Matilda – unless she's really liberated! On the other hand, your lover, your husband or wife, your (selected) friends and some of your family will find it hilarious and in moderately good taste....

Great Britain: Order these super books from your local bookseller or from Exley Publications Ltd, 16 Chalk Hill, Watford, Herts WD1 4BN. (Please send £1.50 to cover post and packing on 1 book, £2.25 on 2 or more books.) Exley Publications reserves the right to show new retail prices on books which may vary from those previously advertised.